12 st
Roger Fuff
September 1955

257-

GERARD MANLEY

HOPKINS

✦✦

SELECTED

POEMS

THE NONESUCH PRESS

66 Chandos Place London WC 2

1954

Printed and made in England

CONTENTS

THE POEMS

WINTER WITH THE GULF STREAM

The boughs, the boughs are bare enough
But earth has never felt the snow.
Frost-furred our ivies are and rough

With bills of rime the brambles shew.
The hoarse leaves crawl on hissing ground
Because the sighing wind is low.

But if the rain-blasts be unbound
And from dank feathers wring the drops
The clogged brook runs with choking sound

Kneading the mounded mire that stops
His channel under clammy coats
Of foliage fallen in the copse.

A simple passage of weak notes
Is all the winter bird dare try.
The bugle moon by daylight floats

So glassy white about the sky,
So like a berg of hyaline,
And pencilled blue so daintily,

I never saw her so divine.
But through black branches, rarely drest
In scarves of silky shot and shine,

The webbed and the watery west
Where yonder crimson fireball sits
Looks laid for feasting and for rest.

I see long reefs of violets
In beryl-covered fens so dim,
A gold-water Pactolus frets

Its brindled wharves and yellow brim,
The waxen colours weep and run,
And slendering to his burning rim

Into the flat blue mist the sun
Drops out and all our day is done.

SPRING AND DEATH

I had a dream. A wondrous thing:
It seem'd an evening in the Spring:
—A little sickness in the air
From too much fragrance everywhere:—
As I walk'd a stilly wood,
Sudden, Death before me stood:
In a hollow lush and damp,
He seem'd a dismal mirky stamp
On the flowers that were seen
His charnelhouse-grate ribs between,
And with coffin-black he barr'd the green.
'Death,' said I, 'what do you here
At this Spring season of the year?'
'I mark the flowers ere the prime
Which I may tell at Autumn-time.'
Ere I had further question made
Death was vanish'd from the glade.
Then I saw that he had bound
Many trees and flowers round
With a subtle web of black,
And that such a sable track
Lay along the grasses green
From the spot where he had been.
   But the Spring-tide pass'd the same;
Summer was as full of flame;
Autumn-time no earlier came.
And the flowers that he had tied,
As I mark'd not always died

Sooner than their mates; and yet
Their fall was fuller of regret:
It seem'd so hard and dismal thing,
Death, to mark them in the Spring.

A SOLILOQUY OF ONE OF THE SPIES
LEFT IN THE WILDERNESS

Who is this Moses? who made him, we say,
To be a judge and ruler over us?
He slew the Egyptian yesterday. To-day
    In hot sands perilous
He hides our corpses dropping by the way
    Wherein he makes us stray.

Your hands have borne the tent-poles: on you plod:
The trumpet waxes loud: tired are your feet.
Come by the flesh-pots: you shall sit unshod
    And break your pleasant meat;
And bring your offerings to a grateful god,
    And fear no law nor rod.

He feeds me with his manna every day:
My soul does loathe it and my spirit fails.
A press of wingèd things comes down this way:
    The gross flock call them quails.
Into my hand he gives a host for prey,
    Come up, Arise and slay.

Sicken'd and thicken'd by the glare of sand
Who would drink water from a stony rock?
Are all the manna-bushes in the land
    A shelter for this flock?
Behold at Elim wells on every hand
    And seventy palms there stand.

5

Egypt, the valley of our pleasance, there!
Most wide ye are who call this gust Simoom.
Your parchèd nostrils snuff Egyptian air,
    The comfortable gloom
After the sandfield and the unveinèd glare!
    Goshen is green and fair.

Not Goshen. Wasteful wide huge-girthèd Nile
Unbakes my pores, and streams, and makes all fresh.
I gather points of lote-flower from an isle
    Of leaves of greenest flesh
Are you sandblind? slabs of water many a mile
    Blaze on him all this while.

In beds, in gardens, in thick plots I stand,
Handle the fig, suck the full-sapp'd vine-shoot.
From easy runnels the rich-piecèd land
    I water with my foot.
Must you be gorged with proof? Did ever sand
    So trickle from your hand?

Strike cymbals, sing, eat, drink, be full of mirth.
Forget the waking trumpet, the long law.
Spread o'er the swart face of this prodigal earth.
    Not manna bring, but straw.
Here are sweet messes without price or worth,
    And never thirst or dearth.

Give us the tale of bricks as heretofore;
To knead with cool feet the clay juicy soil.
Who tread the grapes are splay'd with stripes of gore,

And they who crush the oil
Are spatter'd. We desire the yoke we bore,
   The easy burden of yore.

*   *   *

Go then: I am contented here to lie.
Take Canaan with your sword and with your bow.
Rise: match your strength with monstrous Talmai
   At Kirjath-Arba: go.–
Sure, this is Nile: I sicken, I know not why,
   And faint as though to die.

NEW READINGS

Although the letter said
On thistles that men look not grapes to gather,
  I read the story rather
How soldiers platting thorns around CHRIST'S HEAD
  Grapes grew and drops of wine were shed.

Though when the sower sowed,
The wingèd fowls took part, part fell in thorn,
  And never turned to corn,
Part found no root upon the flinty road –
  CHRIST at all hazards fruit hath shewed.

From wastes of rock He brings
Food for five thousand: on the thorns He shed
  Grains from His drooping Head;
And would not have that legion of winged things
  Bear Him to heaven on easeful wings.

He hath abolished the old drouth,
And rivers run where all was dry,
The field is sopped with merciful dew.
He hath put a new song in my mouth,
The words are old, the purport new,
And taught my lips to quote this word
That I shall live, I shall not die,
But I shall when the shocks are stored
See the salvation of the Lord.

We meet together, you and I,
Meet in one acre of one land,
And I will turn my looks to you,
And you shall meet me with reply,
We shall be sheavèd with one band
In harvest and in garnering,
When heavenly vales so thick shall stand
With corn that they shall laugh and sing.

Where art thou friend, whom I shall never see,
Conceiving whom I must conceive amiss?
Or sunder'd from my sight in the age that is
Or far-off promise of a time to be;
Thou who canst best accept the certainty
That thou hadst borne proportion in my bliss,
That likest in me either that or this,–
Oh! even for the weakness of the plea
That I have taken to plead with, – if the sound
Of God's dear pleadings have as yet not moved thee,–
And for those virtues I in thee have found,
Who say that had I known I had approved thee,–
For these, make all the virtues to abound,–
No, but for Christ who hath foreknown and loved thee.

THE BEGINNING OF THE END : 1

My love is lessened and must soon be past,
I never promised such persistency
In its condition. No, the tropic tree
Has not a charter that its sap shall last
Into all seasons, though no Winter cast
The happy leafing. It is so with me:
My love is less, my love is less for thee.
I cease the mourning and the abject fast,
And rise and go about my works again
And, save by darting accidents, forget.
But ah! if you could understand how then
That " less " is heavens higher even yet
Than treble-fervent " more " of other men,
Even your unpassioned eyelids might be wet.

I must feed fancy. Show me any one
That reads or holds the astrologic lore,
And I'll pretend the credit given of yore;
And let him prove my passion was begun
In the worst hour that's measured by the sun,
With such malign conjunctions that before
No influential heaven ever wore;
That no recorded devilish thing was done
With such a seconding, nor Saturn took
Such opposition to the Lady-star
In the most murderous passage of his book;
And I'll love my distinction: Near or far
He says his science helps him not to look
At hopes so evil-heaven'd as mine are.

THE BEGINNING OF THE END : 3

You see that I have come to passion's end;
This means you need not fear the storms, the cries,
That gave you vantage when you would despise:
My bankrupt heart has no more tears to spend.
Else I am well assured I should offend
With fiercer weepings of these desperate eyes
For poor love's failure than his hopeless rise.
But now I am so tired I soon shall send
Barely a sigh to thought of hopes forgone.
Is this made plain? What have I come across
That here will serve me for comparison?
The sceptic disappointment and the loss
A boy feels when the poet he pores upon
Grows less and less sweet to him, and knows no cause.

THE ALCHEMIST IN THE CITY

My window shows the travelling clouds,
Leaves spent, new seasons, alter'd sky,
The making and the melting crowds:
The whole world passes; I stand by.

They do not waste their meted hours,
But men and masters plan and build:
I see the crowning of their towers,
And happy promises fulfill'd.

And I – perhaps if my intent
Could count on prediluvian age,
The labours I should then have spent
Might so attain their heritage,

But now before the pot can glow
With not to be discover'd gold,
At length the bellows shall not blow,
The furnace shall at last be cold.

Yet it is now too late to heal
The incapable and cumbrous shame
Which makes me when with men I deal
More powerless than the blind or lame.

No, I should love the city less
Even than this my thankless lore;
But I desire the wilderness
Or weeded landslips of the shore.

I walk my breezy belvedere
To watch the low or levant sun,
I see the city pigeons veer,
I mark the lower swallows run

Between the tower-top and the ground
Below me in the bearing air;
Then find in the horizon-round
One spot and hunger to be there.

And then I hate the most that lore
That holds no promise of success;
Then sweetest seems the houseless shore,
Then free and kind the wilderness.

Or ancient mounds that cover bones,
Or rocks where rockdoves do repair
And trees of terebinth and stones
And silence and a gulf of air.

There on a long and squarèd height
After the sunset I would lie,
And pierce the yellow waxen light
With free long looking ere I die.

Myself unholy, from myself unholy
To the sweet living of my friends I look –
Eye greeting doves bright-counter to the rook,
Fresh brooks to salt sand-teasing waters shoaly:

And they are purer, but alas! not solely
The unquestion'd readings of a blotless book.
And so my trust, confusèd, struck, and shook
Yields to the sultry siege of melancholy.

He has a sin of mine, he its near brother,
And partly I hate, partly condone that fall.
This fault in one I found, that in another:

And so, though each have one while I have all,
No " better " serves me now, save " best "; no other
Save Christ: to Christ I look, on Christ I call.

TO OXFORD : 1

New-dated from the terms that reappear,
More sweet-familiar grows my love to thee,
And still thou bind'st me to fresh fealty
With long-superflous ties, for nothing here
Nor elsewhere can thy sweetness unendear.
This is my park, my pleasaunce; this to me
As public is my greater privacy,
All mine, yet common to my every peer.

Those charms accepted of my inmost thought,
The towers musical, quiet-walled grove,
The window-circles, these may all be sought
By other eyes, and other suitors move,
And all like me may boast, impeached not,
Their special-general title to thy love.

TO OXFORD : 2

Thus, I come underneath this chapel-side,
So that the mason's levels, courses, all
The vigorous horizontals, each way fall
In bows above my head, as falsified
By visual compulsion, till I hide
The steep-up roof at last behind the small
Eclipsing parapet; yet above the wall
The sumptuous ridge-crest leave to poise and ride.

None besides me this bye-ways beauty try.
Or if they try it, I am happier then:
The shapen flags and drilled holes of sky,
Just seen, may be to many unknown men
The one peculiar of their pleasured eye,
And I have only set the same to pen.

EASTER COMMUNION

Pure fasted faces draw unto this feast:
God comes all sweetness to your Lenten lips.
You striped in secret with breath-taking whips,
Those crooked rough-scored chequers may be
      pieced
To crosses meant for Jesus; you whom the East
With draught of thin and pursuant cold so nips
Breathe Easter now; you serged fellowships,
You vigil-keepers with low flames decreased,

God shall o'er-brim the measures you have spent
With oil of gladness; for sackcloth and frieze
And the ever-fretting shirt of punishment
Give myrrhy-threaded golden folds of ease.
Your scarce-sheathed bones are weary of being
      bent:
Lo, God shall strengthen all the feeble knees.

See how Spring opens with disabling cold,
And hunting winds and the long-lying snow.
Is it a wonder if the buds are slow?
Or where is strength to make the leaf unfold?
Chilling remembrance of my days of old
Afflicts no less, what yet I hope may blow,
That seed which the good sower once did sow,
So loading with obstruction that threshold
Which should ere now have led my feet to the field.
It is the waste done in unreticent youth
Which makes so small the promise of that yield
That I may win with late-learnt skill uncouth
From furrows of the poor and stinting weald.
Therefore how bitter, and learnt how late, the truth!

My prayers must meet a brazen heaven
And fail or scatter all away.
Unclean and seeming unforgiven
My prayers I scarcely call to pray.
I cannot buoy my heart above;
Above it cannot entrance win.
I reckon precedents of love,
But feel the long success of sin.

My heaven is brass and iron my earth:
Yea iron is mingled with my clay,
So harden'd is it in this dearth
Which praying fails to do away.
Nor tears nor tears this clay uncouth
Could mould, if any tears there were.
A warfare of my lips in truth,
Battling with God, is now my prayer.

c

Let me be to Thee as the circling bird,
Or bat with tender and air-crisping wings
That shapes in half-light his departing rings,
From both of whom a changeless note is heard.
I have found my music in a common word,
Trying each pleasurable throat that sings
And every praised sequence of sweet strings,
And know infallibly which I preferred.
The authentic cadence was discovered late
Which ends those only strains that I approve,
And other science all gone out of date
And minor sweetness scarce made mention of:
I have found the dominant of my range and state –
Love, O my God, to call Thee Love and Love.

THE HALF-WAY HOUSE

Love I was shewn upon the mountain-side
And bid to catch Him ere the drop of day.
See, Love, I creep and thou on wings dost ride:
Love, it is evening now and thou away;
Love, it grows darker here and thou art above;
Love, come down to me if thy name be Love.

My national old Egyptian reed gave way;
I took of vine a cross-barred rod or rood.
Then next I hungered: Love when here, they say,
Or once or never took Love's proper food;
But I must yield the chase, or rest and eat.–
Peace and food cheered me where four rough ways
        meet.

Hear yet my paradox: Love, when all is given,
To see thee I must see thee, to love, love;
I must overtake thee at once and under heaven
If I shall o'ertake thee at last above.
You have your wish; enter these walls, one said:
He is with you in the breaking of the bread.

FOR A PICTURE OF ST. DOROTHEA

I bear a basket lined with grass;
I am so light, I am so fair,
That men must wonder as I pass
And at the basket that I bear,
Where in a newly-drawn green litter
Sweet flowers I carry, — sweets for bitter.

Lilies I shew you, lilies none,
None in Caesar's gardens blow,—
And a quince in hand,— not one
Is set upon your boughs below;
Not set, because their buds not spring;
Spring not, 'cause world is wintering.

But these were found in the East and South
Where Winter is the clime forgot.—
The dewdrop on the larkspur's mouth
O should it then be quenchèd not?
In starry water-meads they drew
These drops: which be they? stars or dew?

Had she a quince in hand? Yet gaze:
Rather it is the sizing moon.
Lo, linkèd heavens with milky ways!
That was her larkspur row. — So soon?
Sphered so fast, sweet soul? — We see
Nor fruit, nor flowers, nor Dorothy.

HEAVEN-HAVEN

A NUN TAKES THE VEIL

I have desired to go
    Where springs not fail,
To fields where flies no sharp and sided hail
    And a few lilies blow.

And I have asked to be
    Where no storms come,
Where the green swell is in the havens dumb,
    And out of the swing of the sea.

THE NIGHTINGALE

'From nine o'clock till morning light
The copse was never more than grey.
The darkness did not close that night
   But day passed into day.
And soon I saw it shewing new
Beyond the hurst with such a hue
As silken garden-poppies do.

'A crimson East, that bids for rain.
So from the dawn was ill begun
The day that brought my lasting pain
   And put away my sun.
But watching while the colour grew
I only feared the wet for you
Bound for the harbour and your crew.

'I did not mean to sleep, but found
I had slept a little and was chill.
And I could hear the tiniest sound,
   The morning was so still –
The bats' wings lisping as they flew
And water draining through and through
The wood: but not a dove would coo.

'You know you said the nightingale
In all our western shires was rare,
That more he shuns our special dale
   Or never lodges there:

26

And I had thought so hitherto –
Up till that morning's fall of dew,
And now I wish that it were true.

'For he began at once and shook
My head to hear. He might have strung
A row of ripples in the brook,
   So forcibly he sung,
The mist upon the leaves have strewed,
And danced the balls of dew that stood
In acres all above the wood.

'I thought the air must cut and strain
The windpipe when he sucked his breath
And when he turned it back again
   The music must be death.
With not a thing to make me fear,
A singing bird in morning clear
To me was terrible to hear.

'Yet as he changed his mighty stops
Betweens I heard the water still
All down the stair-way of the copse
   And churning in the mill.
But that sweet sound which I preferred,
Your passing steps, I never heard
For warbling of the warbling bird.'

Thus Frances sighed at home, while Luke
Made headway in the frothy deep.
She listened how the sea-gust shook
   And then lay back to sleep.

While he was washing from on deck
She pillowing low her lily neck
Timed her sad visions with his wreck.

THE HABIT OF PERFECTION

Elected Silence, sing to me
And beat upon my whorlèd ear,
Pipe me to pastures still and be
The music that I care to hear.

Shape nothing, lips; be lovely-dumb:
It is the shut, the curfew sent
From there where all surrenders come
Which only makes you eloquent.

Be shellèd, eyes, with double dark
And find the uncreated light:
This ruck and reel which you remark
Coils, keeps, and teases simple sight.

Palate, the hutch of tasty lust,
Desire not to be rinsed with wine:
The can must be so sweet, the crust
So fresh that come in fasts divine!

Nostrils, your careless breath that spend
Upon the stir and keep of pride,
What relish shall the censers send
Along the sanctuary side!

O feel-of-primrose hands, O feet
That want the yield of plushy sward,
But you shall walk the golden street
And you unhouse and house the Lord.

And, Poverty, be thou the bride
And now the marriage feast begun,
And lily-coloured clothes provide
Your spouse not laboured-at nor spun.

THE WRECK
OF THE DEUTSCHLAND

To the
happy memory of five Franciscan Nuns
exiles by the Falk Laws
drowned between midnight and morning
of Dec. 7th, 1875

PART THE FIRST

1

Thou mastering me
God! giver of breath and bread;
World's strand, sway of the sea;
Lord of living and dead;
Thou hast bound bones and veins in me, fastened me flesh,
And after it almost unmade, what with dread,
Thy doing: and dost thou touch me afresh?
Over again I feel thy finger and find thee.

2

I did say yes
O at lightning and lashed rod;
Thou heardst me truer than tongue confess
Thy terror, O Christ, O God;
Thou knowest the walls, altar and hour and night:
The swoon of a heart that the sweep and the hurl of thee
      trod
Hard down with a horror of height:
And the midriff astrain with leaning of, laced with fire of
      stress.

31

3

The frown of his face
Before me, the hurtle of hell
Behind, where, where was a, where was a place?
I whirled out wings that spell
And fled with a fling of the heart to the heart of the Host.
My heart, but you were dovewinged, I can tell,
Carrier-witted, I am bold to boast,
To flash from the flame to the flame then, tower from the
      grace to the grace.

4

I am soft sift
In an hourglass – at the wall
Fast, but mined with a motion, a drift,
And it crowds and it combs to the fall;
I steady as a water in a well, to a poise, to a pane,
But roped with, always, all the way down from the tall
Fells or flanks of the voel, a vein
Of the gospel proffer, a pressure, a principle, Christ's gift.

5

I kiss my hand
To the stars, lovely-asunder
Starlight, wafting him out of it; and
Glow, glory in thunder;
Kiss my hand to the dappled-with-damson west:
Since, tho' he is under the world's splendour and wonder,
His mystery must be instressed, stressed;
For I greet him the days I meet him, and bless when I
      understand.

6

Not out of his bliss
Springs the stress felt
Nor first from heaven (and few know this)
Swings the stroke dealt –
Stroke and a stress that stars and storms deliver,
That guilt is hushed by, hearts are flushed by and melt –
But it rides time like riding a river
(And here the faithful waver, the faithless fable and miss).

7

It dates from day
Of his going in Galilee;
Warm-laid grave of a womb-life grey;
Manger, maiden's knee;
The dense and the driven Passion, and frightful sweat;
Thence the discharge of it, there its swelling to be,
Though felt before, though in high flood yet –
What none would have known of it, only the heart, being
       hard at bay,

8

Is out with it! Oh,
We lash with the best or worst
Word last! How a lush-kept plush-capped sloe
Will, mouthed to flesh-burst,
Gush! – flush the man, the being with it, sour or sweet,
Brim, in a flash, full! – Hither then, last or first,
To hero of Calvary, Christ,'s feet –
Never ask if meaning it, wanting it, warned of it – men go.

9

Be adored among men,
God, three-numberèd form;
Wring thy rebel, dogged in den,
Man's malice, with wrecking and storm.
Beyond saying sweet, past telling of tongue,
Thou art lightning and love, I found it, a winter and warm;
Father and fondler of heart thou hast wrung:
Hast thy dark descending and most art merciful then.

10

With an anvil-ding
And with fire in him forge thy will
Or rather, rather then, stealing as Spring
Through him, melt him but master him still:
Whether at once, as once at a crash Paul,
Or as Austin, a lingering-out swéet skíll,
Make mercy in all of us, out of us all
Mastery, but be adored, but be adored King.

PART THE SECOND

11

'Some find me a sword; some
The flange and the rail; flame,
Fang, or flood' goes Death on drum,
And storms bugle his fame.
But wé dream we are rooted in earth – Dust!
Flesh falls within sight of us, we, though our flower the
     same,
Wave with the meadow, forget that there must
The sour scythe cringe, and the blear share come.

12

On Saturday sailed from Bremen,
American-outward-bound,
Take settler and seamen, tell men with women,
Two hundred souls in the round –
O Father, not under thy feathers nor ever as guessing
The goal was a shoal, of a fourth the doom to be drowned;
Yet did the dark side of the bay of thy blessing
Not vault them, the millions of rounds of thy mercy not
      reeve even them in?

Into the snows she sweeps,
Hurling the haven behind,
The Deutschland, on Sunday; and so the sky keeps,
For the infinite air is unkind,
And the sea flint-flake, black-backed in the regular blow,
Sitting Eastnortheast, in cursed quarter, the wind;
Wiry and white-fiery and whirlwind-swivellèd snow
Spins to the widow-making unchilding unfathering deeps.

14

She drove in the dark to leeward,
She struck – not a reef or a rock
But the combs of a smother of sand: night drew her
Dead to the Kentish Knock;
And she beat the bank down with her bows and the ride of
      her keel:
The breakers rolled on her beam with ruinous shock;
And canvas and compass, the whorl and the wheel
Idle for ever to waft her or wind her with, these she
      endured.

15

Hope had grown grey hairs,
Hope had mourning on,
Trenched with tears, carved with cares,
Hope was twelve hours gone;
And frightful a nightfall folded rueful a day
Nor rescue, only rocket and lightship, shone,
And lives at last were washing away:
To the shrouds they took, – they shook in the hurling and
        horrible airs.

16

One stirred from the rigging to save
The wild woman-kind below,
With a rope's end round the man, handy and brave –
He was pitched to his death at a blow,
For all his dreadnought breast and braids of thew:
They could tell him for hours, dandled the to and fro
Through the cobbled foam-fleece, what could he do
With the burl of the fountains of air, buck and the flood of
        the wave?

17

They fought with God's cold –
And they could not and fell to the deck
(Crushed them) or water (and drowned them) or rolled
With the sea-romp over the wreck.
Night roared, with the heart-break hearing a heart-broke
        rabble,
The woman's wailing, the crying of child without check –
Till a lioness arose breasting the babble,
A prophetess towered in the tumult, a virginal tongue told.

36

18

Ah, touched in your bower of bone
Are you! turned for an exquisite smart,
Have you! make words break from me here all alone,
Do you! – mother of being in me, heart.
O unteachably after evil, but uttering truth,
Why, tears! is it? tears; such a melting, a madrigal start!
Never-eldering revel and river of youth,
What can it be, this glee? the good you have there of
      your own?

19

Sister, a sister calling
A master, her master and mine! –
And the inboard seas run swirling and hawling;
The rash smart sloggering brine
Blinds her; but she that weather sees one thing, one;
Has one fetch in her: she rears herself to divine
Ears, and the call of the tall nun
To the men in the tops and the tackle rode over the storm's
      brawling.

20

She was first of a five and came
Of a coifèd sisterhood.
(O Deutschland, double a desperate name!
O world wide of its good!
But Gertrude, lily, and Luther, are two of a town,
Christ's lily and beast of the waste wood:
From life's dawn it is drawn down,
Abel is Cain's brother and breasts they have sucked the
      same.)

37

21

Loathed for a love men knew in them,
Banned by the land of their birth,
Rhine refused them. Thames would ruin them;
Surf, snow, river and earth
Gnashed: but thou art above, thou Orion of light;
Thy unchancelling poising palms were weighing the worth,
Thou martyr-master: in thy sight
Storm flakes were scroll-leaved flowers, lily showers –
         sweet heaven was astrew in them.

22

Five! the finding and sake
And cipher of suffering Christ.
Mark, the mark is of man's make
And the word of it Sacrificed.
But he scores it in scarlet himself on his own bespoken,
Before-time-taken, dearest prizèd and priced –
Stigma, signal, cinquefoil token
For lettering of the lamb's fleece, ruddying of the rose-
         flake.

23

Joy fall to thee, father Francis,
Drawn to the Life that died;
With the gnarls of the nails in thee, niche of the lance, his
Lovescape crucified
And seal of his seraph-arrival! and these thy daughters
And five-livèd and leavèd favour and pride.
Are sisterly sealed in wild waters,
To bathe in his fall-gold mercies, to breathe in his all-fire
         glances.

Away in the loveable west,
On a pastoral forehead of Wales,
I was under a roof here, I was at rest,
And they the prey of the gales;
She to the black-about air, to the breaker, the thickly
Falling flakes, to the throng that catches and quails
Was calling 'O Christ, Christ, come quickly':
The cross to her she calls Christ to her, christens her wild-
       worst Best.

25

The majesty! what did she mean?
Breathe, arch and original Breath.
Is it love in her of the being as her lover had been?
Breathe, body of lovely Death.
They were else-minded then, altogether, the men
Woke thee with a " we are perishing " in the weather of
       Gennesareth.
Or is it that she cried for the crown then,
The keener to come at the comfort for feeling the com-
       bating keen?

26

For how to the heart's cheering
The down-dugged ground-hugged grey
Hovers off, the jay-blue heavens appearing
Of pied and peeled May!
Blue-beating and hoary-glow height; or night, still higher,
With belled fire and the moth-soft Milky Way,
What by your measure is the heaven of desire,
The treasure never eyesight got, nor was ever guessed
       what for the hearing?

No, but it was not these.
The jading and jar of the cart,
Time's tasking, it is fathers that asking for ease
Of the sodden-with-its-sorrowing heart,
Not danger, electrical horror; then further it finds
The appealing of the Passion is tenderer in prayer apart:
Other, I gather, in measure her mind's
Burden, in wind's burly and beat of endragonèd seas.

But how shall I . . . make me room there:
Reach me a . . . Fancy, come faster —
Strike you the sight of it? look at it loom there,
Thing that she . . . there then! the Master,
Ipse, the only one, Christ, King, Head:
He was to cure the extremity where he had cast her;
Do, deal, lord it with living and dead;
Let him ride, her pride, in his triumph, despatch and have
        done with his doom there.

Ah! there was a heart right
There was single eye!
Read the unshapeable shock night
And knew the who and the why;
Wording it how but by him that present and past,
Heaven and earth are word of, worded by? —
The Simon Peter of a soul! to the blast
Tarpeian-fast, but a blown beacon of light.

Jesu, heart's light,
Jesu, maid's son,
What was the feast followed the night
Thou hadst glory of this nun? –
Feast of the one woman without stain.
For so conceivèd, so to conceive thee is done;
But here was heart-throe, birth of a brain,
Word, that heard and kept thee and uttered thee outright.

Well, she has thee for the pain, for the
Patience; but pity of the rest of them!
Heart, go and bleed at a bitterer vein for the
Comfortless unconfessed of them –
No not uncomforted: lovely-felicitous Providence
Finger of a tender of, O of a feathery delicacy, the breast
    of the
Maiden could obey so, be a bell to, ring of it, and
Startle the poor sheep back! is the shipwrack then a
    harvest, does tempest carry the grain for thee?

I admire thee, master of the tides,
Of the Yore-flood, of the year's fall;
The recurb and the recovery of the gulf's sides,
The girth of it and the wharf of it and the wall;
Stanching, quenching ocean of a motionable mind;
Ground of being, and granite of it: past all
Grasp God, throned behind
Death with a sovereignty that heeds but hides, bodes but
    abides;

With a mercy that outrides
The all of water, an ark
For the listener; for the lingerer with a love glides
Lower than death and the dark;
A vein for the visiting of the past-prayer, pent in prison,
The-last-breath penitent spirits – the uttermost mark
Our passion-plungèd giant risen,
The Christ of the Father compassionate, fetched in the
    storm of his strides.

34

Now burn, new born to the world,
Doubled-naturèd name,
The heaven-flung, heart-fleshed, maiden-furled
Miracle-in-Mary-of-flame,
Mid-numbered He in three of the thunder-throne!
Not a dooms-day dazzle in his coming nor dark as he
    came;
Kind, but royally reclaiming his own;
A released shower, let flash to the shire, not a lightning of
    fire hard-hurled.

35

Dame, at our door
Drowned, and among our shoals,
Remember us in the roads, the heaven-haven of the
    Reward:
Our King back, oh, upon English souls!
Let him easter in us, be a dayspring to the dimness of us,
    be a crimson-cresseted east,

More brightening her, rare-dear Britain, as his reign rolls,
Pride, rose, prince, hero of us, high-priest,
Our hearts' charity's hearth's fire, our thoughts' chivalry's
    throng's Lord.

GOD'S GRANDEUR

The world is charged with the grandeur of God.
  It will flame out, like shining from shook foil;
  It gathers to a greatness, like the ooze of oil
Crushed. Why do men then now not reck his rod?
Generations have trod, have trod, have trod;
    And all is seared with trade; bleared, smeared with
        toil;
    And wears man's smudge and shares man's smell:
        the soil
Is bare now, nor can foot feel, being shod.

And for all this, nature is never spent;
  There lives the dearest freshness deep down things;
And though the last lights off the black West went
  Oh, morning, at the brown brink eastward,
      springs –
Because the Holy Ghost over the bent
  World broods with warm breast and with ah! bright
      wings.

THE STARLIGHT NIGHT

Look at the stars! look, look up at the skies!
  O look at all the fire-folk sitting in the air!
    The bright boroughs, the circle-citadels there!
Down in dim woods the diamond delves! the elves'-
        eyes!
The grey lawns cold where gold, where quickgold
        lies!
    Wind-beat whitebeam! airy abeles set on a flare!
    Flake-doves sent floating forth at a farmyard
            scare! –
Ah well! it is all a purchase, all is a prize.

    Buy then! bid then! – What? – Prayer, patience, alms,
        vows.
Look, look: a May-mess, like on orchard boughs!
    Look! March-bloom, like on mealed-with-yellow
            sallows!
These are indeed the barn; withindoors house
The shocks. This piece-bright paling shuts the spouse
    Christ home, Christ and his mother and all his
            hallows.

SPRING

Nothing is so beautiful as spring –
   When weeds, in wheels, shoot long and lovely and
        lush;
   Thrush's eggs look little low heavens, and thrush
Through the echoing timber does so rinse and wring
The ear, it strikes like lightnings to hear him sing;
   The glassy peartree leaves and blooms, they brush
   The descending blue; that blue is all in a rush
With richness; the racing lambs too have fair their fling.

What is all this juice and all this joy?
   A strain of the earth's sweet being in the beginning
In Eden garden. – Have, get, before it cloy,
   Before it cloud, Christ, lord, and sour with sinning,
Innocent mind and Mayday in girl and boy,
   Most, O maid's child, thy choice and worthy the
        winning.

THE LANTERN OUT OF DOORS

Sometimes a lantern moves along the night,
    That interests our eyes. And who goes there?
    I think; where from and bound, I wonder, where,
With, all down darkness wide, his wading light?

Men go by me whom either beauty bright
    In mould or mind or what not else makes rare:
    They rain against our much-thick and marsh air
Rich beams, till death or distance buys them quite.

Death or distance soon consumes them: wind
    What most I may eye after, be in at the end
I cannot, and out of sight is out of mind.

Christ minds; Christ's interest, what to avow or
        amend
    There, éyes them, heart wánts, care haúnts, foot
        fóllows kínd,
Their ránsom, théir rescue, ánd first, fást, last friénd.

47

THE SEA AND THE SKYLARK

On ear and ear two noises too old to end
   Trench – right, the tide that ramps against the
      shore;
   With a flood or a fall, low lull-off or all roar,
Frequenting there while moon shall wear and wend.

Left hand, off land, I hear the lark ascend,
   His rash-fresh re-winded new-skeinèd score
   In crisps of curl off wild winch whirl, and pour
And pelt music, till none's to spill nor spend.

How these two shame this shallow and frail town!
   How ring right out our sordid turbid time,
Being pure! We, life's pride and cared-for crown,

   Have lost that cheer and charm of earth's past
      prime:
Our make and making break, are breaking, down
   To man's last dust, drain fast towards man's first
      slime.

THE WINDHOVER

TO CHRIST OUR LORD

I caught this morning morning's minion, king-
  dom of daylight's dauphin, dapple-dawn-drawn Falcon,
    in his riding
  Of the rolling level underneath him steady air, and
    striding
High there, how he rung upon the rein of a wimpling wing
In his ecstasy! then off, off forth on swing,
  As a skate's heel sweeps smooth on a bow-bend: the
      hurl and gliding
  Rebuffed the big wind. My heart in hiding
Stirred for a bird, – the achieve of, the mastery of the
    thing!

Brute beauty and valour and act, oh, air, pride, plume,
    here
  Buckle! AND the fire that breaks from thee then, a
      billion
Times told lovelier, more dangerous, O my chevalier!

  No wonder of it: shéer plód makes plough down sillion
Shine, and blue-bleak embers, ah my dear,
  Fall, gall themselves, and gash gold-vermilion.

PIED BEAUTY

Glory be to God for dappled things –
   For skies of couple-colour as a brinded cow;
      For rose-moles all in stipple upon trout that
         swim;
Fresh-firecoal chestnut-falls; finches' wings;
   Landscape plotted and pieced – fold, fallow, and
      plough;
   And áll trádes, their gear and tackle and trim.

All things counter, original, spare, strange;
   Whatever is fickle, freckled (who knows how?)
    With swift, slow; sweet, sour; adazzle, dim;
He fathers-forth whose beauty is past change:
         Praise him.

HURRAHING IN HARVEST

Summer ends now; now, barbarous in beauty, the stooks
    arise
  Around; up above, what wind-walks! what lovely
      behaviour
  Of silk-sack clouds! has wilder, wilful-wavier
Meal-drift moulded ever and melted across skies?

I walk, I lift up, I lift up heart, eyes,
  Down all that glory in the heavens to glean our Saviour;
  And, éyes, heárt, what looks, what lips yet gave you a
Rapturous love's greeting of realer, of rounder replies?

And the azurous hung hills are his world-wielding shoulder
  Majestic – as a stallion stalwart, very-violet-sweet! –
These things, these things were here and but the beholder
  Wanting; which two when they once meet,
The heart rears wings bold and bolder
  And hurls for him, O half hurls earth for him off under
    his feet.

THE CAGED SKYLARK

As a dare-gale skylark scanted in a dull cage
    Man's mounting spirit in his bone-house, mean house,
        dwells —
    That bird beyond the remembering his free fells;
This in drudgery, day-labouring-out life's age.

Though aloft on turf or perch or poor low stage,
    Both sing sometimes the sweetest, sweetest spells,
    Yet both droop deadly sómetimes in their cells
Or wring their barriers in bursts of fear or rage.

Not that the sweet-fowl, song-fowl, needs no rest —
Why, hear him, hear him babble and drop down to his
        nest,
    But his own nest, wild nest, no prison.

Man's spirit will be flesh-bound when found at best,
But uncumbered: meadow-down is not distressed
    For a rainbow footing it nor he for his bónes rísen.

IN THE VALLEY OF THE ELWY

I remember a house where all were good
  To me, God knows, deserving no such thing:
  Comforting smell breathed at very entering,
Fetched fresh, as I suppose, off some sweet wood.
That cordial air made those kind people a hood
  All over, as a bevy of eggs the mothering wing
  Will, or mild nights the new morsels of spring:
Why, it seemed of course; seemed of right it should.

Lovely the woods, waters, meadows, combes, vales,
All the air things wear that build this world of Wales;
  Only the inmate does not correspond:
God, lover of souls, swaying considerate scales,
Complete thy creature dear O where it fails,
  Being mighty a master, being a father and fond.

BINSEY POPLARS

FELLED 1879

My aspens dear, whose airy cages quelled,
Quelled or quenched in leaves the leaping sun,
All felled, felled, are all felled;
   Of a fresh and following folded rank
      Not spared, not one
        That dandled a sandalled
      Shadow that swam or sank
On meadow and river and wind-wandering weed-
      winding bank.

   O if we but knew what we do
      When we delve or hew –
    Hack and rack the growing green!
      Since country is so tender
     To touch, her being só slender,
    That, like this sleek and seeing ball
    But a prick will make no eye at all,
    Where we, even where we mean
        To mend her we end her,
      When we hew or delve:
After-comers cannot guess the beauty been.
   Ten or twelve, only ten or twelve
     Strokes of havoc únselve
      The sweet especial scene,
     Rural scene, a rural scene,
     Sweet especial rural scene.

DUNS SCOTUS'S OXFORD

Towery city and branchy between towers;
Cuckoo-echoing, bell-swarmèd, lark-charmèd, rook-
    racked, river-rounded;
The dapple-eared lily below thee; that country and
    town did
Once encounter in, here coped and poisèd powers;

Thou hast a base and brickish skirt there, sours
That neighbour-nature thy grey beauty is grounded
Best in; graceless growth, thou hast confounded
Rural rural keeping – folk, flocks, and flowers.

Yet ah! this air I gather and I release
He lived on; these weeds and waters, these walls are
    what
He haunted who of all men most sways my spirits to
    peace;

Of realty the rarest-veinèd unraveller; a not
Rivalled insight, be rival Italy or Greece;
Who fired France for Mary without spot.

PEACE

When will you ever, Peace, wild wooddove, shy wings shut,
Your round me roaming end, and under be my boughs?
When, when, Peace, will you, Peace? I'll not play
      hypocrite
To own my heart: I yield you do come sometimes; but
That piecemeal peace is poor peace. What pure peace
      allows
Alarms of wars, the daunting wars, the death of it?

O surely, reaving Peace, my Lord should leave in lieu
Some good! And so he does leave Patience exquisite,
That plumes to Peace thereafter. And when Peace here
      does house
He comes with work to do, he does not come to coo,
      He comes to brood and sit.

THE BUGLER'S FIRST COMMUNION

A Bugler boy from barrack (it is over the hill
There) – boy bugler, born, he tells me, of Irish
        Mother to an English sire (he
Shares their best gifts surely, fall how things will),

This very very day came down to us after a boon he on
My late being there begged of me, overflowing
        Boon in my bestowing,
Came, I say, this day to it – to a First Communion.

Here he knelt then in regimental red.
Forth Christ from cupboard fetched, how fain I of feet
        To his youngster take his treat!
Low-latched in leaf-light housel his too huge godhead.

There! and your sweetest sendings, ah divine,
By it, heavens, befall him! as a heart Christ's darling,
        dauntless;
        Tongue true, vaunt- and tauntless;
Breathing bloom of a chastity in mansex fine.

Frowning and forefending angel-warder
Squander the hell-rook ranks sally to molest him;
        March, kind comrade, abreast him;
Dress his days to a dexterous and starlight order.

How it dóes my heart good, visiting at that bleak hill,
When limber liquid youth, that to all I teach
     Yields tender as a pushed peach,
Hies headstrong to its wellbeing of a self-wise self-will!

Then though I should tread tufts of consolation
Dáys áfter, só I in a sort deserve to
     And do serve God to serve to
Just such slips of soldiery Christ's royal ration.

Noting élse is like it, no, not all so strains
Us: fresh youth fretted in a bloomfall all portending
     That sweet's sweeter ending;
Realm both Christ is heir to and thére réigns.

O now well work that sealing sacred ointment!
O for now charms, arms, what bans off bad
     And locks love ever in a lad!
Let mé though see no more of him, and not disappoint-
     ment

Those sweet hopes quell whose least me quickenings
     lift,
In scarlet or somewhere of some day seeing
     That brow and bead of being,
An our day's God's own Galahad. Though this child's
     drift

58

Seems by a divíne doom chánnelled, nor do I cry
Disaster there; but may he not rankle and roam
      In backwheels though bound home? –
That left to the Lord of the Eucharist, I here lie by;

Recorded only, I have put my lips on pleas
Would brandle adamantine heaven with ride and jar,
      did
          Prayer go disregarded:
Forward-like, but however, and like favourable heaven
      heard these.

MORNING MIDDAY AND EVENING
SACRIFICE

The dappled die-away
Cheek and wimpled lip,
The gold-wisp, the airy-grey
Eye, all in fellowship –
This, all this beauty blooming,
This, all this freshness fuming,
Give God while worth consuming.

Both thought and thew now bolder
And told by Nature: Tower;
Head, heart, hand, heel, and shoulder
That beat and breathe in power –
This pride of prime's enjoyment
Take as for tool, not toy meant
And hold at Christ's employment.

The vault and scope and schooling
And mastery in the mind,
In silk-ash kept from cooling,
And ripest under rind –
What life half lifts the latch of,
What hell stalks towards the snatch of,
Your offering, with despatch, of!

THE CANDLE INDOORS

Some candle clear burns somewhere I come by.
I muse at how its being puts blissful back
With yellowy moisture mild night's blear-all black,
Or to-fro tender trambeams truckle at the eye.
By that window what task what fingers ply,
I plod wondering, a-wanting, just for lack
Of answer the eagerer a-wanting Jessy or Jack
There   God to aggrándise, God to glorify.--

Come you indoors, come home; your fading fire
Mend first and vital candle in close heart's vault:
You there are master, do your own desire;
What hinders? Are you beam-blind, yet to a fault
In a neighbour deft-handed? are you that liar
And, cast by conscience out, spendsavour salt?

THE HANDSOME HEART:

AT A GRACIOUS ANSWER

'But tell me, child, your choice; what shall I buy
You?' – 'Father, what you buy me I like best.'
With the sweetest air that said, still plied and pressed,
He swung to his first poised purport of reply.

What the heart is! which, like carriers let fly –
Doff darkness, homing nature knows the rest –
To its own fine function, wild and self-instressed,
Falls light as ten years long taught how to and why.

Mannerly-hearted! more than handsome face –
Beauty's bearing or muse of mounting vein,
All, in this case, bathed in high hallowing grace . . .

Of heaven what boon to buy you, boy, or gain
Not granted! – Only . . . O on that path you pace
Run all your race, O brace sterner that strain!

FELIX RANDAL

Felix Randal the farrier, O he is dead then? my duty all
    ended,
Who have watched his mould of man, big-boned and hardy-
    handsome
Pining, pining, till time when reason rambled in it and
    some
Fatal four disorders, fleshed there, all contended?

Sickness broke him. Impatient he cursed at first, but
    mended
Being anointed and all; though a heavenlier heart began
    some
Months earlier, since I had our sweet reprieve and ransom
Tendered to him. Ah well, God rest him all road ever he
    offended!

This seeing the sick endears them to us, us too it endears.
My tongue had taught thee comfort, touch had quenched
    thy tears,
Thy tears that touched my heart, child, Felix, poor Felix
    Randal;

How far from then forethought of, all thy more boisterous
    years,
When thou at the random grim forge, powerful amidst
    peers,
Didst fettle for the great grey drayhorse his bright and
    battering sandal!

SPRING AND FALL

TO A YOUNG CHILD

Márgarét, are you gríeving
Over Goldengrove unleaving?
Leáves, líke the things of man, you
With your fresh thoughts care for, can you?
Áh! ás the heart grows older
It will come to such sights colder
By and by, nor spare a sigh
Though worlds of wanwood leafmeal lie;
And yet you wíll weep and know why.
Now no matter, child, the name:
Sórrow's springs áre the same.
Nor mouth had, no nor mind, expressed
What heart heard of, ghost guessed:
It ís the blight man was born for,
It is Margaret you mourn for.

64

INVERSNAID

This darksome burn, horseback brown,
His rollrock highroad roaring down,
In coop and in comb the fleece of his foam
Flutes and low to the lake falls home.

A windpuff-bonnet of fáwn-fróth
Turns and twindles over the broth
Of a pool so pitchblack, féll-frówning,
It rounds and rounds Despair to drowning.

Degged with dew, dappled with dew
Are the groins of the braes that the brook treads
        through,
Wiry heathpacks, flitches of fern,
And the beadbonny ash that sits over the burn.

What would the world be, once bereft
Of wet and of wildness? Let them be left,
O let them be left, wildness and wet;
Long live the weeds and the wilderness yet.

9

As kingfishers catch fire, dragonflies dráw flámme;
As tumbled over rim in roundy wells
Stones ring; like each tucked string tells, each hung
     bell's
Bow swung finds tongue to fling out broad its name;
Each mortal thing does one thing and the same:
Deals out that being indoors each one dwells;
Selves — goes itself; "myself" it speaks and spells;
Crying "Whát I dó is me: for that I came."

Í say móre: the just man justices;
Kéeps gráce: thát keeps all his goings graces;
Acts in God's eye what in God's eye he is —
Chríst — for Christ plays in ten thousand places,
Lovely in limbs, and lovely in eyes not his
To the Father through the features of men's faces.

RIBBLESDALE

Earth, sweet Earth, sweet landscape, with leavès throng
And louchèd low grass, heaven that dost appeal
To, with no tongue to plead, no heart to feel;
That canst but only be, but dost that long –

Thou canst but be, but that thou well dost; strong
Thy plea with him who dealt, nay does now deal,
Thy lovely dale down thus and thus bids reel
Thy river, and o'er gives all to rack or wrong.

And what is Earth's eye, tongue, or heart else, where
Else, but in dear and dogged man? – Ah, the heir
To his own selfbent so bound, so tied to his turn,
To thriftless reave both our rich round world bare
And none reck of world after, this bids wear
Earth brows of such care, care and dear concern.

THE LEADEN ECHO
AND THE
GOLDEN ECHO
Maidens' song from St. Winefred's Well

THE LEADEN ECHO

How to kéep – is there ány any, is there none such,
    nowhere known some, bow or brooch or braid or
    brace, láce, latch or catch or key to keep
Back beauty, keep it, beauty, beauty, beauty, . . . from
    vanishing away?
Ó is there no frowning of these wrinkles, rankèd
    wrinkles deep,
Dówn? no waving off of these most mournful messengers,
    still messengers, sad and stealing messengers of
    grey?
No there's none, there's none, O no there's none,
Nor can you long be, what you now are, called fair,
Do what you may do, what, do what you may,
And wisdom is early to despair:
Be beginning; since, no, nothing can be done
To keep at bay
Age and age's evils, hoar hair,
Ruck and wrinkle, drooping, dying, death's worst,
    winding sheets, tombs and worms and tumbling to
    decay;
So be beginning, be beginning to despair.
O there's none; no no no there's none:
Be beginning to despair, to despair,
Despair, despair, despair, despair.

Spare!

There ís one, yes I have one (Hush there!);

Only not within seeing of the sun,

Not within the singeing of the strong sun,

Tall sun's tingeing, or treacherous the tainting of the
earth's air,

Somewhere elsewhere there is ah well where! one,

Oñe. Yes I cán tell such a key, I dó know such a place,

Where whatever's prized and passes of us, everything
that's fresh and fast flying of us, seems to us
sweet of us and swiftly away with, done away
with, undone,

Úndone, done with, soon done with, and yet dearly and
dangerously sweet

Of us, the wimpled-water-dimpled, not-by-morning-
matchèd face,

The flower of beauty, fleece of beauty, too too apt to,
ah! to fleet,

Never fleets móre, fastened with the tenderest truth

To its own best being and its loveliness of youth: it is an
everlastingness of, O it is an all youth!

Come then, your ways and airs and looks, locks, maiden
gear, gallantry and gaiety and grace,

Winning ways, airs innocent, maiden manners, sweet
looks, loose locks, long locks, lovelocks, gaygear,
going gallant, girlgrace –

Resign them, sign them, seal them, send them, motion
them with breath,

And with sighs soaring, soaring síghs deliver

69

F

Them; beauty-in-the-ghost, deliver it, early now, long
      before death
Give beauty back, beauty, beauty, beauty, back to God,
      beauty's self and beauty's giver.
See; not a hair is, not an eyelash, not the least lash lost;
      every hair
Is, hair of the head, numbered.
Nay, what we had lighthanded left in surly the mere
      mould
Will have waked and have waxed and have walked with
      the wind what while we slept,
This side, that side hurling a heavyheaded hundredfold
What while we, while we slumbered.
O then, weary then why should we tread? O why are we
      so haggard at the heart, so care-coiled, care-
      killed, so fagged, so fashed, so cogged, so
      cumbered,
When the thing we freely fórfeit is kept with fonder a
      care,
Fonder a care kept than we could have kept it, kept
Far with fonder a care (and we, we should have lost it)
      finer, fonder
A care kept. – Where kept? Do but tell us where kept,
      where. –
Yonder. – What high as that! We follow, now we follow.
      – Yonder, yes yonder, yonder,
Yonder.

SPELT FROM SIBYL'S LEAVES

Earnest, earthless, equal, attuneable, * vaulty,
    voluminous, . . . stupendous
Evening strains to be tíme's vást, * womb-of-all, home-
    of-all, hearse-of-all night.
Her fond yellow hornlight wound to the west, * her wild
    hollow hoarlight hung to the height
Waste; her earliest stars, earl-stars, * stárs principal,
    overbend us,
Fíre-féaturing heaven. For earth * her being has
    unbound, her dapple is at an end, as-
tray or aswarm, all throughther, in throngs; * self ín self
    steepèd and páshed – quíte
Disremembering, dísmémbering * áll now. Heart, you
    round me right
With: Óur évening is over us; óur night * whélms,
    whélms, ánd will end us.
Only the beak-leaved boughs dragonish * damask the
    tool-smooth bleak light; black,
Ever so black on it. Óur tale, O óur oracle! * Lét life,
    wáned, ah lét life wind
Off hér once skéined stained véined varíety * upon, áll
    on twó spools; párt, pen, páck
Now her áll in twó flocks, twó folds – black, white; *
    right, wrong; reckon but, reck but, mind
But thése two; wáre of a wórld where bút these * twó
    tell, each off the óther; of a rack
Where, selfwrung, selfstrung, sheathe- and shelterless, *
    thóughts agaínst thoughts ín groans grínd.

THE SOLDIER

Yes. Whý do we áll, seeing of a soldier, bless him? bless
Our redcoats, our tars? Both these being, the greater part,
But frail clay, nay but foul clay. Here it is: the heart,
Since, proud, it calls the calling manly, gives a guess
That, hopes that, makesbelieve, the men must be no less;
It fancies, feigns, deems, dears the artist after his art;
And fain will find as sterling all as all is smart,
And scarlet wear the spirit of wár thére express.

Mark Christ our King. He knows war, served this soldier-
    ing through;
He of all can reeve a rope best. There he bides in bliss
Now, and séeing somewhére some mán do all that man can
    do,
For love he leans forth, needs his neck must fall on, kiss,
And cry 'O Christ-done deed! So God-made-flesh does
    too:
Were I come o'er again' cries Christ 'it should be this'.

CARRION COMFORT

Not, I'll not, carrion comfort, Despair, not feast on thee;
Not untwist – slack they may be – these last strands of
    man
In me ór, most weary, cry "I can no more." I can;
Can something, hope, wish day come, not choose not to be.
But ah, but O thou terrible, why wouldst thou rude on me
Thy wring-world right foot rock? lay a lionlimb against
    me? scan
With darksome devouring eyes my bruisèd bones? and fan,
O in turns of tempest, me heaped there; me frantic to avoid
    thee and flee?

    Why? That my chaff might fly; my grain lie, sheer and
    clear.
Nay in all that toil, that coil, since (seems) I kissed the rod,
Hand rather, my heart lo! lapped strength, stole joy,
    would laugh, chéer.
Cheer whom though? the hero whose heaven-handling
    flung me, fóot tród
Me? or me that fought him? O which one? is it each one?
    That night, that year
Of now done darkness I wretch lay wrestling with (my
    God!) my God.

No worst, there is none. Pitched past pitch of grief,
More pangs will, schooled at forepangs, wilder wring.
Comforter, where, where is your comforting?
Mary, mother of us, where is your relief?
My cries heave, herds-long; huddle in a main, a chief
Woe, world-sorrow; on an age-old anvil wince and
    sing —
Then lull, then leave off. Fury had shrieked 'No ling-
ering! Let me be fell: force I must be brief'.

O the mind, mind has mountains; cliffs of fall
Frightful, sheer, no-man-fathomed. Hold them cheap
May who ne'er hung there. Nor does long our small
Durance deal with that steep or deep. Here! creep,
Wretch, under a comfort serves in a whirlwind: all
Life death does end and each day dies with sleep.

74

¶

I wake and feel the fell of dark, not day.
What hours, O what black hoürs we have spent
This night! what sights you, heart, saw; ways you
    went!
And more must, in yet longer light's delay.
    With witness I speak this. But where I say
Hours I mean years, mean life. And my lament
Is cries countless, cries like dead letters sent
To dearest him that lives alas! away.

    I am gall, I am heartburn. God's most deep decree
Bitter would have me taste: my taste was me;
Bones built in me, flesh filled, blood brimmed the
    curse.
    Selfyeast of spirit a dull dough sours. I see
The lost are like this, and their scourge to be
As I am mine, their sweating selves; but worse.

Patience, hard thing! the hard thing but to pray,
But bid for, Patience is! Patience who asks
Wants war, wants wounds; weary his times, his tasks;
To do without, take tosses, and obey.

   Rare patience roots in these, and, these away,
Nowhere. Natural heart's ivy, Patience masks
Our ruins of wrecked past purpose. There she basks
Purple eyes and seas of liquid leaves all day.

   We hear our hearts grate on themselves: it kills
To bruise them dearer. Yet the rebellious wills
Of us we do bid God bend to him even so.
   And where is he who more and more distils
Delicious kindness? – He is patient. Patience fills
His crisp combs, and that comes those ways we know.

My own heart let me more have pity on; let
Me live to my sad self hereafter kind,
Charitable; not live this tormented mind
With this tormented mind tormenting yet.
   I cast for comfort I can no more get
By groping round my comfortless, than blind
Eyes in their dark can day or thirst can find
Thirst's all-in-all in all a world of wet.

Soul, self; come, poor Jackself, I do advise
You, jaded, let be; call off thoughts awhile
Elsewhere; leave comfort root-room; let joy size
At God knows when to God knows what; whose smile
's not wrung, see you; unforeseen times rather – as
    skies
Betweenpie mountains – lights a lovely mile.

THAT NATURE IS A HERACLITEAN FIRE AND
OF THE COMFORT OF THE RESURRECTION

Cloud-puffball, torn tufts, tossed pillows * flaunt forth,
    then chevy on an air-
built thoroughfare: heaven-roysterers, in gay-gangs *
    they throng; they glitter in marches.
Down roughcast, down dazzling whitewash, * wherever an
    elm arches,
Shivelights and shadowtackle in long * lashes lace, lance,
    and pair.
Delightfully the bright wind boisterous * ropes, wrestles,
    beats earth bare
Of yestertempest's creases; * in pool and rut peel parches
Squandering ooze to squeezed * dough, crust, dust;
    stanches, starches
Squadroned masks and manmarks * treadmire toil there
Footfretted in it. Million-fuelèd, * nature's bonfire burns
    on.
But quench her bonniest, dearest * to her, her clearest-
    selvèd spark
Man, how fast his firedint, * his mark on mind, is gone!
Both are in an unfathomable, all is in an enormous dark
Drowned. O pity and indig * nation! Manshape, that
    shone
Sheer off, disseveral, a star, * death blots black out; nor
    mark
        Is any of him at all so stark
But vastness blurs and time * beats level. Enough! the
    Resurrection,
A heart's-clarion! Away grief's gasping, * joyless days,
    dejection.

Across my foundering deck shone

A beacon, an eternal beam. * Flesh fade, and mortal trash

Fall to the residuary worm; * world's wildfire, leave but
ash:

In a flash, at a trumpet crash,

I am all at once what Christ is, * since he was what I am,
and

This Jack, joke, poor potsherd, * patch, matchwood, immortal diamond,

Is immortal diamond.

ST. ALPHONSUS RODRIGUEZ

LAYBROTHER OF THE SOCIETY OF JESUS

Honour is flashed off exploit, so we say;
And those strokes once that gashed flesh or galled shield
Should tongue that time now, trumpet now that field,
And, on the fighter, forge his glorious day.
On Christ they do and on the martyr may;
But be the war within, the brand we wield
Unseen, the heroic breast not outward-steeled,
Earth hears no hurtle then from fiercest fray.

   Yet God (that hews mountain and continent,
Earth, all, out; who, with trickling increment,
Veins violets and tall trees makes more and more)
Could crowd career with conquest while there went
Those years and years by of world without event
That in Majorca Alfonso watched the door.

¶

JUSTUS QUIDEM TU ES DOMINE SI DISPUTEM
TECUM: VERUMTAMEN JUSTA LOQUAR AD TE:
QUARE VIA IMPIORUM PROSPERATUR? Etc.

Thou art indeed just, Lord, if I contend
With thee; but, sir, so what I plead is just.
Why do sinners' ways prosper? and why must
Disappointment all I endeavour end?
　　Wert thou my enemy, O thou my friend,
How wouldst thou worse, I wonder, than thou dost
Defeat, thwart me? Oh, the sots and thralls of lust
Do in spare hours more thrive than I that spend,
Sir, life upon thy cause. See, banks and brakes
Now, leavèd how thick! lacèd they are again
With fretty chervil, look, and fresh wind shakes
Them; birds build – but not I build; no, but strain,
Time's eunuch, and not breed one work that wakes.
Mine, O thou lord of life, send my roots rain.

5

Why should their foolish bands, their hopeless hearses
Blot the perpetual festival of day?
Ravens, for prosperously-boded curses
Returning thanks, might offer such array.
Heaven comfort sends, but harry it away,
Gather the sooty plumage from Death's wings
And the poor corse impale with it and fray
Far from its head an angel's hoverings.
And count the rosy cross with bann'd disastrous
    things.

It was a hard thing to undo this knot.
The rainbow shines but only in the thought
Of him that looks. Yet not in that alone,
For who makes rainbows by invention?
And many standing round a waterfall
See one bow each, yet not the same to all,
But each a hand's breadth further than the next.
The sun on falling waters writes the text
Which yet is in the eye or in the thought.
It was a hard thing to undo this knot.

EPIGRAM

Of virtues I most warmly bless,
Most rarely seen, Unselfishness.
And to put graver sins aside,
I own a preference for Pride.

¶

    I am like a slip of comet,
Scarce worth discovery, in some corner seen
Bridging the slender difference of two stars,
Come out of space, or suddenly engender'd
By heady elements, for no man knows;
But when she sights the sun she grows and sizes
And spins her skirts out, while her central star
Shakes its cocooning mists; and so she comes
To fields of light; millions of travelling rays
Pierce her; she hangs upon the flame-cased sun,
And sucks the light as full as Gideon's fleece:
But then her tether calls her; she falls off,
And as she dwindles shreds her smock of gold
Between the sistering planets, till she comes
To single Saturn, last and solitary;
And then she goes out into the cavernous dark.
So I go out: my little sweet is done:
I have drawn heat from this contagious sun:
To not ungentle death now forth I run.

Now I am minded to take pipe in hand
And yield a song to the decaying year;
Now while the full-leaved hursts unalter'd stand,
    And scarcely does appear

The Autumn yellow feather in the boughs
    While there is neither sun nor rain;
And a gray heaven does the hush'd earth house,
And bluer gray the flocks of trees look in the plain.

So late the hoar green chestnut breaks a bud,
And feeds new leaves upon the winds of Fall;
So late there is no force in sap or blood;
    The fruit against the wall
Loose on the stem has done its summering;
These should have starv'd with the green broods of
       spring,
    Or never been at all;
Too late or else much, much too soon,
Who first knew moonlight by the hunter's moon.

¶

How looks the night? There does not miss a star.
The million sorts of unaccounted motes
Now quicken, sheathed in the yellow galaxy.
There is no parting or bare interstice
Where the stint compass of a skylark's wings
Would not put out some tiny golden centre.

Moonless darkness stands between.
Past, O Past, no more be seen!
But the Bethlehem star may lead me
To the sight of Him who freed me
From the self that I have been.
Make me pure, Lord: Thou are holy;
Make me meek, Lord: Thou wert lowly;
Now beginning, and alway:
Now begin, on Christmas day.

The earth and heaven, so little known,
Are measured outwards from my breast.
I am the midst of every zone
And justify the East and West;

The unchanging register of change
My all-accepting fixèd eye,
While all things else may stir and range
All else may whirl or dive or fly.

The swallow, favourite of the gale,
Will on the moulding strike and cling,
Unvalve or shut his vanèd tail
And sheathe at once his leger wing.

He drops upon the wind again;
His little pennon is unfurled.
In motion is no weight or pain,
Nor permanence in the solid world.

There is a vapour stands in the wind;
It shapes itself in taper skeins:
You look again and cannot find,
Save in the body of the rains.

And these are spent and ended quite;
The sky is blue, and the winds pull
Their clouds with breathing edges white
Beyond the world; the streams are full

And millbrook-slips with pretty pace
Gallop along the meadow grass. –
O lovely ease in change of place!
I have desired, desired to pass . . .

MOONRISE

I awoke in the Midsummer not to call night, * in the white
    and the walk of the morning:
The moon, dwindled and thinned to the fringe * of a finger-
    nail held to the candle,
Or paring of paradisaïcal fruit, * lovely in waning but
    lustreless,
Stepped from the stool, drew back from the barrow, * of
    dark Maenefa the mountain;
A cusp still clasped him, a fluke yet fanged him, *
    entangled him, not quit utterly.
This was the prized, the desirable sight, * unsought, pre-
    sented so easily,
Parted me leaf and leaf, divided me, * eyelid and eyelid of
    slumber.

CHEERY BEGGAR

Beyond Mágdalen and by the Bridge, on a place called
  there the Plain,
  In Summer, in a burst of summertime
  Following falls and falls of rain,
When the air was sweet-and-sour of the flown fineflower of
Those goldnails and their gaylinks that hang along a lime;

  The motion of that man's heart is fine
  Whom want could not make píne, píne
That struggling should not sear him, a gift should cheer
  him
Like that poor pocket of pence, poor pence of mine.

¶

Repeat that, repeat,
Cuckoo, bird, and open ear-wells, heart-springs, delight-
     fully sweet,
With a ballad, with a ballad, a rebound
Off trundled timber and scoops of the hillside ground,
      hollow hollow hollow ground:
The whole landscape flushes on a sudden at a sound.

¶

The times are nightfall, look, their light grows less;
The times are winter, watch, a world undone:
They waste, they wither worse; they as they run
Or bring more or more blazon man's distress.
And I not help. Nor word now of success:
All is from wreck, here, there, to rescue one –
Work which to see scarce so much as begun
Makes welcome death, does dear forgetfulness.

Or what is else? There is your world within.
There rid the dragons, root out there the sin.
Your will is law in that small commonweal . . .

Thee, God, I come from, to thee go,
All day long I like fountain flow
From thy hand out, swayed about
Mote-like in thy mighty glow.

What I know of thee I bless,
As acknowledging thy stress
On my being and as seeing
Something of thy holiness.

Once I turned from thee and hid,
Bound on what thou hadst forbid;
Sow the wind I would; I sinned:
I repent of what I did.

Bad I am, but yet thy child.
Father, be thou reconciled,
Spare thou me, since I see
With thy might that thou art mild.

I have life before me still
And thy purpose to fulfil;
Yea a debt to pay thee yet:
Help me, sir, and so I will.

But thou bidst, and just thou art,
Me shew mercy from my heart
Towards my brother, every other
Man my mate and counterpart.

. . . . .

95

ON THE PORTRAIT OF TWO BEAUTIFUL YOUNG PEOPLE

A BROTHER AND SISTER

O I admire and sorrow! The heart's eye grieves
Discovering you, dark tramplers, tyrant years.
A juice rides rich through bluebells, in vine leaves,
And beauty's dearest veriest vein is tears.

Happy the father, mother of these! Too fast:
Not that, but thus far, all with frailty, blest
In one fair fall; but, for time's aftercast,
Creatures all heft, hope, hazard, interest.

And are they thus? The fine, the fingering beams
Their young delightful hour do feature down
That fleeted else like day-dissolvèd dreams
Or ringlet-race on burling Barrow brown.

She leans on him with such contentment fond
As well the sister sits, would well the wife;
His looks, the soul's own letters, see beyond,
Gaze on, and fall directly forth on life.

But ah, bright forelock, cluster that you are
Of favoured make and mind and health and youth,
Where lies your landmark, seamark, or soul's star?
There's none but truth can stead you. Christ is truth.

There's none but good can bé good, both for you
And what sways with you, maybe this sweet maid;

None good but God – a warning wavèd to
One once that was found wanting when Good
    weighed.

Man lives that list, that leaning in the will
No wisdom can forecast by gauge or guess,
The selfless self of self, most strange, most still,
Fast furled and all foredrawn to No or Yes.

Your feast of; that most in you earnest eye
May but call on your banes to more carouse.
Worst will the best. What worm was here, we cry,
To have havoc-pocked so, see, the hung-heavenward
    boughs?

Enough: corruption was the world's first woe.
What need I strain my heart beyond my ken?
O but I bear my burning witness though
Against the wild and wanton work of men.

    .   .   .   .   .   .

EPITHALAMION

Hark, hearer, hear what I do; lend a thought now, make
  believe
We are leafwhelmed somewhere with the hood
Of some branchy bunchy bushybowered wood,
Southern dene or Lancashire clough or Devon cleave,
That leans along the loins of hills, where a candycoloured,
  where a gluegold-brown
Marbled river, boisterously beautiful, between
Roots and rocks is danced and dandled, all in froth and
  water-blowballs, down.
We are there, when we hear a shout
That the hanging honeysuck, the dogeared hazels in the
  cover
Makes dither, makes hover
And the riot of a rout
Of, it must be, boys from the town
Bathing: it is summer's sovereign good.

By there comes a listless stranger: beckoned by the noise
He drops towards the river: unseen
Sees the bevy of them, how the boys
With dare and with downdolphinry and bellbright bodies
  huddling out,
Are earthworld, airworld, waterworld thorough hurled, all
  by turn and turn about.

This garland of their gambols flashes in his breast
Into such a sudden zest
Of summertime joys

98

That he hies to a pool neighbouring; sees it is the best
There; sweetest, freshest, shadowiest;
Fairyland; silk-beech, scrolled ash, packed sycamore, wild
      wychelm, hornbeam fretty overstood
By. Rafts and rafts of flake-leaves light, dealt so, painted
      on the air,
Hang as still as hawk or hawkmoth, as the stars or as the
      angels there,
Like the thing that never knew the earth, never off roots
Rose. Here he feasts: lovely all is! No more: off with –
      down he dings
His bleachèd both and woolwoven wear:
Careless these in coloured wisp
All lie tumbled-to; then with loop-locks
Forward falling, forehead frowning, lips crisp
Over finger-teasing task, his twiny boots
Fast he opens, last he offwrings
Till walk the world he can with bare his feet
And come where lies a coffer, burly all of blocks
Build of chancequarrièd, selfquainèd rocks
And the water warbles over into, filleted with glassy grassy
      quicksilvery shivès and shoots
And with heavenfallen freshness down from moorland still
      brims,
Dark or daylight on and on. Here he will then, here he will
      the fleet
Flinty kindcold element let break across his limbs
Long. Where we leave him, froliclavish, while he looks
      about him, laughs, swims.

Enough now; since the sacred matter that I mean
I should be wronging longer leaving it to float

99

Upon this only gambolling and echoing-of-earth note –
What is . . . the delightful dene?
Wedlock. What is water? Spousal love.

Father, mother, brothers, sisters, friends
Into fairy trees, wild flowers, wood ferns
Rankèd round the bower

INDEX OF FIRST LINES

101

H

102

103

Of this edition 1100 copies have been printed by
the Stellar Press of Barnet on rag paper in the
Times Bold type for sale in the United Kingdom
by the Nonesuch Press of London and in Canada
and the United States through Max Reinhardt
(Canada) Ltd of Toronto. The wood-engraving
on the title page is by Kenneth Lindley, the
binding by Mansell of London. The text is that
of the third Oxford edition, edited by W. H.
Gardner and here used by arrangement with
Geoffrey Cumberlege, Oxford University Press.
The poems have been chosen and the book de-
signed by Francis Meynell.

The Bodleian MS of "The Wreck of the
Deutschland" is, except for one verse, in the
hand not of Hopkins but of Robert Bridges. As
the Bridges MS arrangement is not consistent in
its indenting and does not conform to the rhyme
scheme, the editor has felt free to indulge his
preference for alignment by the left.

This is number 299